The Mind Hackers Guide To Detecting Lies

"How to instantly and accurately recognize when someone is lying."

James G Springer

"The Mind Hackers Guide to Detecting Lies"

Springer Technologies, LLC

Copyright © 2019 by James G. Springer

All rights reserved. No part of this book may be used or reproduced by any means, graphic, electronic or mechanical, including photocopying, recording, taping or by any information storage retrieval system without the written permission of the publisher except in the case of brief quotations embodied in critical articles and reviews.

«Acknowledgements»

To my beautiful wife, who has stood by me through thick and thin, in good times and bad, for better and for worse. She's believed in me since the start and many times when I didn't believe in myself.

To my children, who, though grown and on their own continue to be an inspiration to me and a driving force that keeps me moving forward.

My parents, for always believing in me, encouraging me and never letting me give up on myself. Of all the parents in the world, if given the chance, I'd pick you. The example you set for me is a high standard that I can only hope and pray I'll someday live up to.

« Introduction » 1

« Chapter 1 » Who Lies? 5
    The Purpose of This Book 6
    Will This Make Me a Better Liar 7
    Chapter Summary 7

« Chapter 2 » Why is Detecting Lies Important? 9
    Business Lies 9
    Lies in Personal Life 10
    Everyone's a Liar 10
    The Truth Always Leaks Out 11
    Symmetry is Everything 11
    Baselining to Prove a Lie 12
    The Four Primary Reasons We Lie 13
    The Types of Lies We Tell 14
    Statistics about lies 18
    Chapter Summary 19

The Science 21

« Chapter 3 » The Mind Science Behind Deception 23
    Why Mind Science is Important to You 23
    Processing Capacity – Conscious vs. Subconscious 25
    Mind Speed – Conscious vs. Subconscious 28
    How Freely Do You Think? 29
    Thinking versus Remembering 30
    The Reticular Activating System (RAS) 32
    The Emotional Refractory Period 33
    The Transderivational Search 34
    Your Three Brains 35
    Chapter Summary 38

« Chapter 4 » Your Reptile Brain 39
Where is the Reptilian R-Complex? 39
What does the "R-Complex" (Reptile Brain) do? 40
The Reptile Brain and Social Status 42
The Four Things You Must Understand 44
The Reptile Dance 45
Chapter Summary 46

« Chapter 5 » Your Emotional Brain 49
Where is the Emotional Limbic System? 49
The Neural Network 50
Living in the Rut 52
Thoughts, Emotions and Behavioral Patterns 53
Pleasure vs. Pain 53
State Control 54
Chapter Summary 56

« Chapter 6 » Your Human Brain 59
Where is the Logical, Rational Neocortex? 59
What does the Neocortex do? 60
The Lying Brain 62
Chapter Summary 62

Introduction to Deception Analysis 65

« Chapter 7 » Deception Analysis 67
The Truth About Catching Lies 67
Chapter Summary 69

« Chapter 8 » Nonverbal Communication 71
The Body Speaks 71

It's not what you say, but how you say it 72
Chapter Summary 73

Hot Spots 75

« Chapter 9 » Lying by Comparison 77
What is Lying by Comparison? 77
The Process 78
Chapter Summary 79

« Chapter 10 » Verbal Indications of Deception 81
What are Verbal Hot Spots? 81
Verbal Hot Spots 83
Chapter Summary 99

« Chapter 11 » Physical Indicators of Deception 101
What do we look for when detecting lies? 102
Physical Hot Spots 104
Chapter Summary 117

« Chapter 12 » Micro Expressions 119
What are Micro Expressions? 119
The Seven Universal Expressions of Emotion 120
Types of Emotional Displays 121
Chapter Summary 122

« Conclusion » 123

« Introduction »

In my first book I outlined in considerable detail my story of origin, but I feel it's important that my readers understand who I am, where I came from, and what I've been through that brought me to the point of writing this book.

I was born in poverty in a small town in southern Indiana. What my parents couldn't supply with money they more than made up for with the love that always surrounded us. Over the years of my childhood I watched my parents claw and fight their way into the middle class before I graduated high school. The lessons of overcoming I witnessed by watching my parents shaped much of my adult life. I learned that life is possible and can be enjoyed with little means. I learned that where you are is where you are, but it doesn't mean you can't change and make life better.

After being medically discharged from the United States Air Force I was lost. I had lost the career I had counted on having for the rest of my life before it had even begun. I was lost and a little jaded. I knew I didn't want to go to a four-year college, ut had to do something. The Air Force paid for me to go to Technical College, so I studied to become a design engineer. I hated that job. I worked my way into the computer networking side of the business and became a network administrator. I hated that job as well. I hated being stuck in an office doing the same thing over and over and having my livelihood dangling from the strings held by my employer. At 28 I had had enough and started my first company. In three years, I built that company from less than zero, to over a million dollars per year in sales and then watched it come completely apart. The failure of that company cost me everything I had. Fortunately, Indiana is a homestead state, so I did manage to keep my house.

Within one month of the books closing on my destruction I started another company. By the time I reached 34 I had built the company into a nice multimillion-dollar company contracting with the Department of Defense. Budget cuts required me to make the decision to take my money and retire.

Unfortunately, I had made some very bad investment decisions and lost everything I had again which forced me back into the job market. Over the following years I worked for a number of companies in a wide variety of industries managing and training sales professionals. Over the course of thirty plus years I sold or managed well in excess of $100 million in sales, probably closer to $200 million in today's money.

In the past 10 years I've been diagnosed with five chronic illnesses, a mental illness, and had a severe car accident. Needless to say, going through that has caused some much-needed changes in my life. When I was diagnosed as a Type 2 Diabetic (one of my chronic illnesses) I asked the doctor what I had to do to get well. Her response is what triggered the turnaround in my life. If you ever want to have a bad day at the doctor's office…just find yourself asking your doctor how you're going to get well and have them tell you, "You will never be well. For you there is no "well", only "management". According to my doctor I should have died by my fiftieth birthday. As of the date of this writing I'm fifty-five.

These three events sparked in me a thirst for knowledge about the human mind and sent me on a quest for answers.

As a result, I have spent tens of thousands of dollars and hours learning about the human mind. What makes it work and why it does the things it does and how to effectively change it. I accidentally stumbled onto deception and micro expression analysis through a course I took on controlling the human mind to manage pain. My skill set not only helped me to manage my injuries and illnesses but gave me a greater insight into human behavior, not the least of which is learning to recognize when I'm being lied to *and* to see the emotions of others that they try to hide.

I was always frustrated by the fact that clients, prospects, the people I worked for, the people who worked for me, trusted friends and even family had lied to me, only to find out too late to take any action.

Learning to see when someone is lying is a powerful skill to possess but it's a two-edged sword. While it is nice to have the ability to see when someone is trying to directly hurt you with a lie, it is equally as frustrating to see the frequency with which everyone I encounter lies.

I came to terms with that though and have learned to not just see the lies but understand why a person would lie to me. I have also come to the point that while I see lies all the time, to discount and leave the liar be.

We are lied to between 8 and 200 times per day. If I were to call out every lie I catch, that's all I would be doing. It's also fun when people discount my abilities and think I don't see their deception when in reality I do.

I hope you enjoy this book and learn how exciting it can be to accurately, instantly recognize when and how you're being lied to. This book will not make you an expert deception analyst, but it will put you worlds beyond the average person you encounter every day.

« Chapter 1 »
Who Lies?

One of the most fascinating and powerful things I teach has to be the ability to accurately detect when someone is lying. Regardless of social status, race, color or creed. No matter what religion anyone is, they all have one thing in common. They are all liars.

We all lie, in fact, we all lie a lot. You may think you don't, but research shows that all people are in fact liars. Think about the last time someone asked you how you were doing. Were you honest and told them how you're actually doing, or did you tell the number one lie told and say, "I'm fine", in some form? You see we all do, in fact, lie quite regularly.

What makes detecting lies, or, deception analysis, interesting is that not only do we all lie, but we're really bad at it, as well. Lying is not natural, yet everyone does it quite regularly. Lying requires conscious, deliberate action. We must first think of the truth, and then create a lie to negate the truth. Once we create the lie, we then have to remember it, preferably as we told it. Next, we must create a cover story to back up the lie. Once we create the cover story, we then must create another lie to cover that lie as well.

The conscious mind can only process and track between, 5 to 7 "bits" of information at one time. When we lie, we create a condition called Cognitive Overload, which means the conscious mind can no longer accurately process the information required to lie. Obviously, it takes much longer to describe the process than it takes to perform it. The entire process can happen anywhere from a fraction of a second to two seconds, depending on the type and gravity of the lie being told

The Purpose of This Book

In this book we'll look at the ways in which people lie, and how to quickly and accurately detect them. This book is not exhaustive and will not make you a professional deception analyst. It will, however, give you a huge advantage in negotiations and conversations when recognizing lies and how to respond to people when they lie.

Additionally, we'll go into some of the "mind science" that will help you understand where lies are formed and why deception is nearly always detectable to the trained eye and ear.

The most important things to understand and what I will show you in this book are:

1. Everyone lies.

2. Everyone lies differently

3. Most of the time each individual will lie in the same way dependent on the gravity of the lie.

4. How lies are formed in the mind.

5. It's not "if" someone lies, but rather, "why" they are lying.

My goal in this book is to show you, not only how to detect deception but also that detecting deception is based in science and not parlor tricks or luck. It's important to know how to handle the situation when someone lies. The goal in deception analysis is not only to detect deception, but to ultimately get to the truth.

Will This Make Me a Better Liar

No. Learning to detect lies will not make you a better liar. You may become more aware of your own deception indicators or "hot spots", but you will be no better at covering them than someone who has no training.

Chapter Summary

The primary purpose of this book is to teach you the basics of human lie detection. Everyone lies and most people lie the same even though everyone lies differently.

The primary reason deception analysis, or human lie detection works is that most lies put a person in a state of cognitive overload in which case the subconscious intervenes and leaks the truth.

Remember, the question is not IF someone has lied, but rather WHY they've lied. The goal is not to catch a lie, but to find the truth.

« Chapter 2 »
Why is Detecting Lies Important?

The ability to accurately detect when someone is lying is an incredibly valuable skill to possess. Beyond its importance…it is also very fun. Detecting lies is also somewhat of a two-edged sword. It is truly valuable but can also be somewhat discouraging as you watch your friends, family and colleagues lie to you.

Business Lies

In business we've all faced deception. In fact, 100% of all business transactions include deception of some sort. Approximately 60% of all job applicants lie on their CV or résumé. I imagine you, yourself, have been involved with business transactions, whether it be, selling a product or service, interviewing a potential new hire, company meetings, asking for a raise, and a host of other business "transactions", where after the fact you realized that you had been lied to.

Business lies range from insignificant, where there is little or no cost, to catastrophic, where thousands even millions of dollars are lost.

It only makes sense then that the ability to detect lies is a skill worth having to protect you and your business from those who would deceive you for their own gain or to your detriment.

Lies in Personal Life

The ability to accurately detect lies is equally important in your personal life, as well.

If you're single and dating, have you ever found someone to be less than honest when arranging that first date? That's because approximately 90% of all people lie on their dating profile.

What about your family life? Do your family members lie to you? Well, statistics show that 86% of all people lie regularly to their parents. Do you have siblings? 73% of all people lie regularly to their siblings, and 69% lie regularly to their spouse.

Kind of sheds a new light on the importance of being able to detect lies. Does it not?

Everyone's a Liar

So, who lies? Everyone; everybody lies. Regardless of your race, religion, socioeconomics, or any other category you choose, we all lie. We all lie, we lie a lot and we're very bad at it. Lying is not a natural thing for the human mind to do. Therefore, it makes lies relatively easy to spot if you know what to look for.

When I'm speaking and say that everyone lies, I generally get some pushback from at least some of the people in the audience who believe they are 100% honest in all things. It's important, however, to remember that anything that's not 100% the truth is 100% a lie. In fact, the number one most told lie is, "I'm fine" or some form of that statement.

The Truth Always Leaks Out

In deception analysis we are not looking for lies, but rather we are looking for the truth. Nearly all Hot Spots are actually the truth subconsciously leaking out. That is what we're looking for...truth.

Lying causes what's known as "cognitive overload" in the mind. This overload causes a disconnect between the conscious and subconscious mind. When this occurs, the subconscious mind will "leak" the truth, or at least signal the deception analyst something is wrong. These are often called "hot spots".

We'll cover more on cognitive overloading and what happens inside the mind of the liar in much more detail later in the book.

Even though some Hot Spots have a very high likelihood of indicating a lie by themselves it is important to note that no one Hot Spot proves the person is lying. It is best to have three, but no less than two depending on the value assigned to the Hot Spot.

Symmetry is Everything

Nearly every gesture or facial expression is symmetrical. There are a few exceptions, but for the most part the right side of the body or face should mirror the left.

When looking for deception asymmetry is a big indicator that something is wrong with the story you're hearing.

When a person is lying the resulting cognitive overload often results in an asymmetrical facial expression or gesture. The person is consciously trying to control their movements, but the subconscious is already starting to perform the gesture or expression.

Baselining to Prove a Lie

The most accurate method of proving a person is lying is through baselining. Most teaching on deception will tell you to baseline only truthful behavior; however, if you want to improve on your accuracy you should also baseline a person's deceptive behavior, as well. This is accomplished by using three types of questions.

1. Casual Questions (get the person relaxed)
2. Control Questions (get the person to lie to non-relevant questions)
3. Relevant Questions (the questions that matters to the analyst)

By using these three types of questions you can gauge not only a person's honest behavior, but you can also gain valuable insight as to how that person behaves when lying. Everybody lies differently, but every individual typically lies the same.

If a person slightly shrugs one shoulder when asked a control question (a question to which you know they will likely lie, but has no relevance to the situation); they will likely lie the same way when confronted with a Relevant Question (a question to which they might lie and is important to the situation).

The gravity, or importance, of the lie will typically result in a variance in display of the hot spots. The lie, "I'm fine", has very little gravity, should the person be found to have lied. However, the question, "Have you ever cheated on your wife", could have tremendous gravity depending on the context in which it was asked.

When you ask a Relevant Question, it is important to notice any change in body movement or speech. The 80 plus hot spots mentioned in this book are not the only ones. Any unusual or atypical behavior when confronted with a question (relevant or control) can indicate deception.

It is also important to note that when using this method, it is critically important that the person be allowed to return to their truthful relaxed state. In other words, you cannot follow a control question with a relevant question and get an accurate read on that person's deceptive behaviors. Plus, it would be a little awkward in an interview.

Unfortunately, in most scenarios we don't have the luxury of a formal interview setting. Most of the lies you see are spontaneous lies told during normal conversation. It is for this reason knowing even the basics of deception analysis can be a huge advantage for you. Remember, the goal in deception analysis is not finding the lie, it's uncovering the truth.

The Four Primary Reasons We Lie

There are any number of reasons why we lie but here are four of the most common ones.

They are:

1. To make someone else look better

2. To make our self look better

3. To protect someone else

4. To protect ourselves

We often lie to help someone else look better in certain situations. You may say something such as "Bob would make a great addition to our team", when in fact you know he probably wouldn't, but you want to help your friend by making him look better than he really is.

The same is true when trying to make our self look better. You might tell a perspective employer that you're always on time for work, when in fact, you have issues with punctuality but don't want to be judged by your past record.

You may also try to protect someone by lying. You might tell your boss, "Jane called me from the road yesterday. She was stuck in traffic, which is why she was late." You know she overslept, but in order to protect her you lied.

Finally, and this is the most important, we lie to protect ourselves from the consequences of our actions. When asked, "Do you use the company car for personal use?" And you reply, "I would never do that." Even though you do occasionally use it to run an errand or two rather than rearrange the cars in your driveway. It's a small thing to you, but a violation of corporate policy, so you lie to protect yourself from the consequences of your actions.

The Types of Lies We Tell

We tell many types of lies but here are some of the most common lies we tell.

1. White Lies
2. Lies of Exaggeration
3. Lies of Omission

4. Half Truths

5. Direct Deception

White Lies –

The most common lies told are the "Little White Lies". The most common white lie told is "I'm fine". Our world could be coming apart, but we lie rather than tell someone the truth.

Or, it could be "The store was out of 2% milk, so I bought whole milk," when there was plenty of 2% but the person buying it wanted whole milk instead.

These lies are of little or no value. And while it is always best to tell the truth, and it is true that all lies have consequences, most of the time the liar feels it's worth telling the lie.

Lies of Exaggeration –

Lies of exaggeration are very common. These lies may be low value lies, or they can be very high value depending on context. You see lies of exaggeration everywhere. They are common when using numbers or globalizations in describing something.

An applicant in a job interview might say, "I always give 100% to whatever I do." That is a lie of exaggeration because no one does. Studies have shown that as many as 60% of all job applicants lie on their résumé. These lies are often lies of exaggeration. People lie about how much money they've made in the past, their job performance, how long they were employed and when they were employed.

Lies of Omission –

Lies of omission are also very common. They are often moderate to high value lies. Many times, when the truth would hurt us or maybe someone else, we will conveniently leave out some of the details. Everything we say is the truth, but overall is a lie because we left out critical information.

A man might tell his wife that on his way home he stopped and got gas, went to the grocery, then came home. When in fact between the gas and the grocery he stopped and spent $100 on lottery tickets. Everything he said was the truth…he just left out a small part of the story to cover his behavior.

Half Truths –

The half-truth is often seen in political and corporate speeches and meetings. The liar believes that by sandwiching a lie within the truth, the lie will be more believable.

A politician might say, "Social Security funding is a major issue, it is very important to me and is of great importance to all those who will soon retire". The truth is that Social Security funding IS a major issue and is of great importance to those who will soon retire. The lie is in the middle of the sentence. "…is very important to me…" He may have no interest in Social Security Funding, but he knows his constituents feel it's very important, so he sandwiches a lie between two true statements.

Direct Deception or "Bald Face Lie" –

Direct deception is commonly a very high value lie. It takes a lot of guts to look someone in the eye and intentionally try to deceive them. It also causes the most conflict between the conscious and subconscious mind. Therefore, it results in the greatest and most noticeable hot spots when you know what to look and listen for.

If you are interviewing a salesperson and you ask them if they've ever intentionally called on another salesperson's prospects, the answer will likely be the same, or at least to the untrained interviewer it would appear to be the same.

An honest person would simply say "No". A deceptive person might say, "I would never contact another salesperson's prospect, that would be unethical and I'm a very ethical person". Just in the verbiage alone there are hot spots all over the place, not to mention what their body is doing as they answer.

If the interviewer is trained, he or she will recognize the deception immediately. At that point, the interviewer might offer to ask the question again in a slightly different manner, or tactfully call the person out by saying, something such as, "your response and body language are telling me something different when you answered that question. Let me put it another way…"

Statistics about lies.

As I stated earlier, we all lie, we lie a lot, and we do it very badly. Here are some statistics that demonstrate just how prolific at lying we are. These statistics are the excepted norms in the industry.

- 60% of all people average 2.92 lies per 10 minutes of conversation

- 90% of children have grasped the concept of lying by age 4

- The average person is lied to 8 to 20 times per day

- 100% of all business transactions include deception

- 90% of all online dating profiles contain lies

- 86% of all people regularly lie to their parents

- 75% of all people regularly lie to their friends

- 73% of all people regularly lie to their siblings

- 69% of all people regularly lie to their spouse

- 50-60% of all job applicants lie on their résumé'(depending on the study you use)

- Men lie the most at 3 to 8 times per day

- Women 1 to 5 times per day

- Teen age girls lie the most, averaging 3 to 10 lies per day.

- The more popular the person the more they lie and the better they are at it.

- The most prolific documented liar in history – President Richard Nixon @ 837 lies in one day

Chapter Summary

In this chapter you learned that EVERYONE is a liar. Remember that anything that is not completely true is completely a lie. The most common lie told is, "I'm Fine" or some derivation of the phrase.

You now know that we also lie a lot, but are very bad at it when in the company of a trained deception analyst.

One thing not mentioned earlier is that while human lie detection is as good or better than electronic lie detectors, and a lot more practical, no one can detect 100% of the lies they're told. The average for someone fully trained is about 85%. Considering most people MISS 80% of the lies they're told when not looking for deception and only catch around 54% when specifically looking for deception, the percentage is pretty good.

The Science

« Chapter 3 »
The Mind Science Behind Deception

In this chapter we're going to look into the constructs of the human mind. We'll look at the mind's capacity, speed differences between certain parts of the mind and the responsibilities of these parts. We'll discover which part of the brain is responsible for creating lies and why it's so bad at it.

Why Mind Science is Important to You

It may seem strange to take a deep dive into brain science when discussing deception analysis (spotting lies). It is not, however, I assure you. Most of us have taken a very misguided approach to catching lies. People tend to believe that:

1. They are good at detecting lies without specific training.

I have been told on countless occasions by well-meaning but, ignorant people, they are already good at spotting lies, when in fact, they are no better than the average person on the street. The truth is, an untrained person will, when looking for a lie, catch around 54% of the lies they're told. When not specifically looking for a lie they will miss 80% of the lies they're told.

2. They believe deception detection is a parlor trick that uses shills in order to appear to have a special power.

We've all seen staged shows by "mentalists" who seem to have the power to magically read people's mind. Some use science and some are staged. True deception analysis is not a parlor trick it's based purely on science and interpreting the subconscious clues we all demonstrate in a given context.

3. They don't believe it's possible to accurately detect lies in real time while having a normal conversation.

Most people I've met don't really believe it's actually possible to detect deception in real time conversation. They may believe it's possible to some degree in a formal interrogation where the conditions are setup to catch a person lying. In fact, once a person has been trained it is fairly easy to pick up on the between 8 and 200 lies you're told every day. Once you understand the science behind deception analysis, it becomes automatic just like any other skill.

More has been learned about the human brain in the last 50 years than in the previous 5,000. The more we learn how the human mind functions the more we can learn to see how it manifests itself through behavior. The more we learn how the mind affects the body the more readily we can recognize when the subconscious is speaking louder than the persons words.

I know many will see this chapter and roll their eyes because they think "Science is Boring". And I'll grant you many sciences as taught by academia are boring. I personally hated science when I was in school. But that's because it seemed to me the science had no purpose. It was all numbers, formulas and theories, but at the end of the day it had no value for me. I couldn't see how learning the periodic table was going to help me in life.

This science, however, is different. This science, at least to me, is fascinating. I wanted, no, I *needed* to understand as much about the human mind as I possibly could. With my diagnosis of mental illness, and the injury I sustained in a major car accident, it was important to me to understand how the mind works and why we do the things we do. I don't have all the answers, that's for certain. In fact, I know that with all I've learned there's much more that I don't know than what I do know. And I know a lot.

If you take the time to read this complete chapter as it lays out the functions and processes of the mind, I believe you will be glad you did. Some of it you may know, but I'd be willing to bet, most of it you don't.

So, let's open up the human mind and see what the driving science is behind the ability to detect lies.

Processing Capacity – Conscious vs. Subconscious

Although both the conscious and unconscious mind has amazing power, there are some important differences that we need to understand. Both have strengths and weaknesses. We have already discussed the fact that the subconscious is much faster at processing information. We are now going to look at the capacity of each to handle input or stimuli and the difference is vast. We are constantly being bombarded by stimulus information that we deal with in a variety of ways. In computer terms, it is estimated that we are receiving about 2 to 4 million bits of information per second. I've seen estimates much higher, but 2.4 million bits per second is a widely used number. Regardless of what the actual number may be, it is an amazingly large amount of data for us to handle, but the subconscious does it with ease. This in comparison to the 5-7bits of information the conscious mind is capable of processing. (More on that later)

The subconscious mind has the capacity to take in all the data to which we are exposed and records everything. Although not all the information we receive is recorded...it is not necessarily directly retrievable by the conscious mind it is stored for as long as we live. This hidden information stored in the subconscious is likely still used in forming opinions, associations and to "fill in the blanks" when data is missing or not known with certainty when making decisions. The subconscious mind's ability to fill in the blanks is one of the many means by which the subconscious makes its incredibly fast decisions.

Our powerful subconscious minds require only a fraction of a second to make determinations about others. These determinations are nearly impossible to change and are usually accurate. In less than a second of someone coming into your view (no need to speak to or hear them), your subconscious mind will determine if that person is trustworthy and likeable along with several other personality assessments. This is based largely on long-term memory, associations and emotions. When you see the person your subconscious begins to fill in the blanks about them regarding critical characteristics about that person. This is a part of our survival mechanism. The fraction of a second assessment is hardwired in us as a means of threat assessment and comes largely from the most primitive part of our mind.

Conversely, the conscious mind is the executive part of our mind and has incredible problem-solving capabilities. It is responsible for language, mathematical skills, analysis and other critical thought. However, it is limited in its ability to effectively handle multiple informational input or stimuli. On average, the conscious mind of most people has the capacity to deal with between 5 to 7 bits, or chunks, of information plus or minus 2. Therefore, some people can only handle 3 bits/chunks of information while others may go as high as 9 bits/chunks. We will go into greater detail on this process in a later chapter when we discuss this part of the brain specifically.

Once the conscious mind's ability to process information is exceeded the person will become overwhelmed and will typically escape into a state known as "fight/flight". While it may not make sense right now, there are times when an effective, powerful communicator can benefit from putting the person with whom they are engaged into a state of overwhelmed. Therefore, the conscious mind tends to filter out things that do not seem important at the time. The conscious mind deletes, distorts and generalizes information constantly. This process allows the conscious mind to avoid being overwhelmed, leaving the task of dealing with the vast amount of information being received to the subconscious mind.

The majority of this information goes completely unnoticed by our conscious mind because of its limited capacity to cognitively deal with multiple stimulus. These things are a part of your immediate environment, yet your conscious mind is completely oblivious to them. However, your subconscious mind was not. It notices everything both inside and outside of you.

Mind Speed – Conscious vs. Subconscious

Another important factor to understand about mind science is the speed at which both parts of the mind operate. The brain is an amazing organ whose processing power is unmatched by anything ever created by man. The speed at which our minds operate is staggering. Our conscious mind operates incredibly fast, but it pales in comparison to the blistering speed at which the subconscious mind operates. Our subconscious mind operates approximately 1.5 times faster than the conscious mind. Even though we are talking about fractions of a second in many cases this speed differential is vital in the way we make decisions and process information.

Whenever information or stimulus is received a race begins between the conscious and unconscious mind. The outcome of this race is always the same. The subconscious always wins. The reason I mention this is that even when presented with information that appears to be cognitive the subconscious mind still reacts first. This is one of the reasons why a logical decision to act in a specific way is often met with resistance. Even though the action would make logical sense and is in the best interest of the person, the subconscious mind grabbed the information first and assigned some unfavorable emotion, association or threat assessment to the information before it can be analyzed cognitively.

When we understand this there is great advantage to the effective communicator. The biggest advantage is the fact that the subconscious mind does not have the capacity to deceive. Therefore, if we know what and *how* to look for subconscious signals, we can gain great insight into the actual feelings, emotions and truth in the person with whom we are communicating. These subconscious leaks cannot be controlled consciously because once the slower conscious mind recognizes it, it is too late.

These subconscious signals can be extremely subtle and difficult to recognize consciously if you don't know what to look for. However, these responses and reactions to them are so primitively wired into our minds, they are often subconsciously perceived, as well. Have you ever met with a person and what they said sounded good, logical and beneficial, but you just had a "bad feeling" about the person? Most likely, this is caused by the fact that your primitive subconscious mind has picked up on their subconscious cues. Your subconscious may have picked up on subtle subconscious behavior incongruent with their verbal message, and then overrides your cognitive desire to accept that person's verbal message.

How Freely Do You Think?

As the highest member of the food chain, we humans like to think ourselves to be rational, analytical thinkers. We believe ourselves to have free choice, and to be somewhat unpredictable. However, that is not the case. In fact, the more unpredictable we try to be the more predictable we become. If, for example, I were to ask you to count to five on your fingers I can predict with nearly 100% accuracy how you will do it. Nearly everyone in the United States will begin with a closed fist and start counting by extending the index finger. That is not true if you are from another culture. For example, if you are Japanese you would most likely start with an open hand and start counting by closing the fingers from the little finger through the thumb. In America, if I asked you to think of a flower, about 80% of you would choose a rose as your first choice. In playing cards, most women choose the Queen of Hearts, while men choose the Ace of Spades. I could go through dozens of these exercises to prove to you that we are not as unpredictable as we think.

These are simple examples of a much more complex mechanism. You could choose to begin counting on any finger, but you most likely chose to start with your index finger. You could have chosen any flower, but odds are you picked a rose. However, regardless of which finger, or flower you chose, you chose it without cognitive thought, the actions or images happened automatically. This is a result of how your brain makes decisions.

Thinking versus Remembering

As I stated previously, we tend to mistakenly believe we are highly evolved, rational, critical and logical thinkers. What most of us confuse for thinking is technically remembering. The human brain has an incredible ability to utilize past experiences. We quickly analyze new stimuli, take that new information and run it through past experiences and associations, then generate a response by comparison to what is already known.

If you were badly scared or bitten by a dog when you were a young child, the mere thought of the word dog, will generate a negative mental image and association regardless of context. The more these feelings and associations are reinforced the stronger they become, to the point that it is extremely difficult to change. This happens in both negative and positive experience or associations.

These associations drive our behavior at a subconscious level. The subconscious mind is a safety mechanism. Its primary purpose is to protect us and provide good things for us. Unfortunately, the associations that are made in the subconscious are not necessarily best for us long term. Consider the person who is addicted to drugs or alcohol. The addict has created powerfully positive associations with the drug. They may know that the behavior is destructive cognitively, however, when the subconscious and the conscious minds conflict, the subconscious mind will win almost every time. The only way to change the behavior is to change the subconscious associations and feelings about the behavior. Appealing to the person's logic will not change the behavior. Many times, you will hear about addicts who didn't change until they "hit rock bottom". When this happens, the persons, positive associations are radically and almost instantly changed. Once the associations are changed, the addiction can be much more easily overcome. Obviously, there are sometimes chemical dependencies that must be dealt with. However, when the pleasure association is overcome, the pain of dealing with the chemical dependency is much easier to overcome.

Whether a person is addicted to a chemical or a behavior the process is the same. The neuropathways in that person's mind is driving the behavior, not logic. Changing a person's feeling about spiders is the same as changing their feelings about a product or service. When you make a sales presentation to a prospect, it is imperative to learn how that prospect feels about the product/service in general, plus what if any beliefs or associations they may have regarding you, your brand or your company. You could be selling the best car, with the best safety record that holds its value and is very affordable. However, if your prospect or someone they know was involved in a bad accident in that model of car, they very well may have a powerful negative association to that vehicle. The person could have also been influenced by someone whose opinion they value or read an article in a trusted publication that forms a negative association.

Now, imagine sitting across from a person who had a friend who was seriously injured in that vehicle, that after the accident they were told by someone they trust that, that vehicle is not safe, that they then go on the internet and check how many times that vehicle is involved in serious accidents. This person is going to have a very powerful negative association and belief regarding the vehicle even if the information they have received is flawed or more likely skewed. It is likely that no matter what you say or show the person they will not see anything other than what they want to see.

The Reticular Activating System (RAS)

The RAS is what your brain uses to determines internal or subconscious focus. You don't necessarily notice that it's directing your focus, but it is without question. This is why some people seem to have opportunities or money comes to them all the time while someone else has nothing but lack and want.

A great example of the way the emotional refractory system works is in purchasing a new car. If you've ever bought a new car, you have likely experienced this.

You go to some auto dealerships. You look at a wide variety of makes and models of vehicles in the process. At some point, you find that "perfect" vehicle. Many times, a vehicle you have not seen a lot of on the road, making your purchase somewhat special.

You buy your vehicle and take off down the road but something interesting comes to your attention. Suddenly, it seems that everyone in your area bought the very same vehicle that day. You begin seeing the vehicle you just purchased everywhere!

Why does this happen? It is because the reticular activating system has changed your internal emotional filters which changes what you notice. Before your purchase you had no emotional association to that vehicle. Now you own one. which creates an emotional connection. This emotional shift causes your mind to filter for that vehicle, thus you notice them whenever you meet one. There are no more of those vehicles on the road, you have simply begun noticing them.

The Emotional Refractory Period

The psychological mechanism of reflection through refraction is referred to as the "emotional refractory period". Logic and rational analysis have nothing to do with this. It is purely subconscious. Dr. Paul Ekman in his book "Emotions Revealed", makes much of the refractory period of emotions. The refractory period can vary from a few moments to a lifetime. What is important to note is the power it has over our ability to make objective decisions because the refractory system that filters what we see or perceive.

Emotions have a life cycle or half-life. When you go into a state like anger, your mind naturally wants to remain in that state. And however long it can keep the Emotional Refractory Period looking for ways to hold on to that feeling, will determine the length of the Emotional Refractory Period.

For example, have you ever had a heated argument with someone? In the end, you come to some resolution. However, even though the issue has been resolved, when you see that person, or hear that person talking down the hall, you instantly return to that state. We also see the Emotional Refractory Period at work on the other end of the spectrum. Say, you meet someone to whom you are very attracted. You meet them and everything goes great. So great, that you find yourself in a state near euphoria by being with that person. The next day while going about your regular routine you "happen" to think of that person, and instantly you feel those same feelings start to well up. You text them and they text you back and the state strengthens. Then you talk on the phone and ask them out and they say yes, and the state or feelings become even stronger. You may find that the feelings are even stronger than when you originally met. That's how the Emotional Refractory period works.

The Transderivational Search

The method by which you make these determinations is not cognitive. It is a subconscious function called a transderivational search and you have no control over how it works. If, for example, If I were to make the statement:

"The Dog Was Blue"

When I made the statement, your mind went through a transderivational search for "dog". It searched your memory banks through every instance of "dog" in your life from beginning to end. It then compared all those instances, and then pulled the one it felt most likely to fit the context it then created a mental picture of the one it chose. Not knowing what was coming next it likely pulled the one that was the most powerful memory, Perhaps, a childhood pet, a favorite dog memory, or even a dog that attacked you at some point in your life. This happens almost instantaneously and creates a picture of a dog in your mind. What it most likely did not do is create a picture of a "Blue" dog. Statements like this cause what we call mental friction because they require the cognitive mind to stop the process, engage, and change the "Black Lab", or whatever the dog you created, into a blue dog. The blue dog may not even be the same breed. It may now be a Beagle or a Border collie.

Additionally, if we had compounded the friction by stating:

"The Dog Was Blue and Bit Me"

We have now caused another stop point. Our first dog was a friendly Black Lab that had to suddenly be changed into a friendly "Blue Beagle". Now we have to stop again because the dog is no longer friendly. We now have to make our Blue Dog a biting dog, so once again we have to change our mental picture of the dog to one that bites, so now it is a different dog again.

But what if we add even more to the statement and were to say:

"The Dog Was Blue and Bit Me Viciously"

Now once again we must change the dog. Not only did it bite me, but it bit me viciously. So, in this short sentence we have had to change the color of the dog once, the breed of the dog once, but most likely twice, and the temperament of the dog at least two and possibly three times, all requiring conscious engagement in order to do so. However, had we simply ordered the words correctly we could have done so in a way that would have required very minimal if any conscious effort. All we would have had to do would be to make the statement read:

"I Was Viciously Bitten by The Blue Dog"

By speaking in this way, you automatically reduce or eliminate "Mental Friction". This allows you to quickly, easily bypass the other person's conscious mind, the part of the mind which utilizes words, logic and reason. Once you bypass the critical, conscious mind you move your communication directly to the subconscious mind which uses only pictures, feelings, emotions and survival instincts.

Your Three Brains

We tend to think of our brain as one single organ. However, you actually have three brains that make up the one. They are the Reptilian Brain (Reticulated Cortex or R-

Complex), the Paleomammalian Brain (Limbic System), and the Neomammalian Brain (Neocortex)

Each of these "brains" brings different characteristics and functions to the table. The Neomammalian Brain (the largest part of our brain) is the "human" brain, or the logical, thinking brain. It is the part of the mind in charge of executive thought, analysis and problem solving.

The Paleomammalian Brain (the second largest) is the emotional brain. It controls and manages feelings, associations and long-term memory storage and recall.

The Reptilian Brain (the smallest part of our brain) is primarily responsible for our survival and the propagation of our gene pool. It controls the autonomic nervous system by regulating such things as body temperature, blood pressure, breathing, and all other bodily functions necessary to survive. It is also designed to protect us from outside threats by altering the autonomic nervous system to prepare the body for and executes the freeze / flight / fight response. This part of the brain also controls our primal drives to stay fed, and find a mate, which means that social status is important to the reptile brain, because historically, social status directly related to importance and mating preference within the group.

These three brains while providing unique and differing functions communicate and interact continuously sending and receiving information from one to the other. While it is true that all three parts work together, the fact that each is responsible for different functions means that they are often at odds with each other. Often the Reptilian and Mammalian Brains gang up on the Human Brain, because they are much faster and have much higher computational power. This creates a hierarchy in the decision-making process that is extremely important to understand, and most people get it entirely wrong.

Logic would tell us that the largest part of the brain, the Neomammalian, or neocortex, the part responsible for logical, critical and analytical thought would be the dominant part of the brain when it comes to making decisions. However, that is not the case. Studies have shown that it is the Reptilian or R-Complex that has the primary say, then the Paleomammalian (Limbic System). These two make between 96 and 98% of all decisions. Only 2 to 4% of the decisions we make are made logically. That is not theory that is neuroscience.

Another important thing to note about the three parts of the brain is how they present externally through our body movements and language. Those of us who are specifically trained in body language, micro expressions and human deception detection use the knowledge of how the brain processes information. We use that information to recognize signals of stress and anxiety, hidden and subtle emotions, honesty and deception. While this book will not make you an expert, by the time you complete this text you will know more about how we receive, process and act on information than most of the people you know. By using this information, you can begin to become substantially better at accurately predicting how a person will respond to nearly any stimuli. The more you practice and use this information the more accurate you will become at predicting human behavior. The power to predict or respond to hidden or subtle human behavior means you can quickly adapt your communication strategies to make the likelihood of a positive outcome much greater.

In the following chapters, we will look at each of these parts of the brain in more detail demonstrating the significance each plays in the decision-making process. We will discuss how to communicate with each of the different parts of the brain and when it is advantageous to do so.

It sounds complicated I know, but it will become much clearer as we continue through the "Inside Out" process. Let's proceed through the human mind from the inside out beginning with the oldest, smallest, yet very powerful R-Complex of the brain commonly referred to as the "Reptilian" or "Lizard" brain.

Chapter Summary

The goal of this chapter was to give you a basic understanding of how the mind processes information and how each of the three parts of the brain contribute in our ability to detect lies.

The next three chapters will each deal with one specific area of the mind. This will help you better understand what each part does and an even greater understanding of the hierarchy and how the "three brains" interact.

In the next chapter, we will begin our journey through the three brains. Our first stop will be the "basement", the most primitive and powerful region of the mind. The "Reptile".

« Chapter 4 »
Your Reptile Brain

Scientific Name: Reticulated Cortex or the R-Complex

Common Names – "Reptile Brain", "Lizard Brain"

Primary Functions – Survival / Autonomic Function

Decision Making Hierarchy – Highest

Capacity to Lie - None

Where is the Reptilian R-Complex?

The "R-Complex" or "Reptile Brain" is the oldest part of the brain. Whether you believe in evolution or creation matters not. Either way this part of the brain is the oldest and most primitive because it is the part that forms first and performs the most primitive functions in human beings. It is also the only part of the brain that we share with every vertebrate species of animal on the planet. This is why it is this region of the brain that is commonly called the "Reptile" or "Lizard" brain. The reptilian part of the brain performs virtually the same functions in lizards, humans and every other species of vertebrate animals.

The R-Complex or reptile brain was originally considered to consist of the brain stem and the cerebellum. Most people today consider the amygdala to be a part of the reptilian brain structure as well, although it is also very interactive with the Limbic System or "Mammalian Brain". The amygdala is the primary sentry of our brain. It never shuts off. The amygdala is constantly assessing our environment for anything that could harm us. Even when your body is sleeping, your mind is processing, and the amygdala is paying attention. If you have ever gone from deep sleep to instantly awake and attentive it is the amygdala that's responsible for jolting the reptilian brain and waking you up, most likely in a state of Freeze/Flight/Fight.

What does the "R-Complex" (Reptile Brain) do?

Even though this is the smallest of the three regions of the brain it is extraordinarily powerful and without it life would be impossible. This little part of our brains is responsible for your autonomic nervous system. The reptile brain controls such things as your breathing, your heart rate, regulates your body temperature, blood pressure and all the other automatic functions of the body that don't require conscious thought. There are automatic functions in which you can consciously intervene. You don't have to consciously tell your eyes to blink, they do so automatically. You can, however, consciously blink your eyes. You breathe automatically, but you can also consciously change your breathing. By the same token, you can consciously decide to scratch your nose, which would not appear to be autonomic, but in certain cases it becomes so.

It is important to understand that the autonomic nervous system contains two subsystems. These are the sympathetic and parasympathetic nervous systems. It is the reptile brain that determines whether we remain in homeostasis (a state of physiological balance or equilibrium).

When we are relaxed and experiencing minimal stress we remain in homeostasis. In homeostasis, the Parasympathetic Nervous System is in control. When we experience elevated stress or anxiety, the Sympathetic Nervous System takes over. Both sides of the autonomic nervous system play an important role. Both can be beneficial, and both can be detrimental depending on context.

When the Parasympathetic Nervous System is in control you will experience specific physiology. Some of the key physiological results of being under the control of the Parasympathetic are:

Eye Pupils Contracted	Stimulates Peristalsis (digestion)
Stimulates Saliva	Stimulates Gallbladder
Slows Heart Rate	Contracts the Bladder
Constricts Bronchi	Relaxes the Rectum
	Peripheral Vasodilation

Generally, in this state you will feel more balanced, more creative, more comfortable, persuasive and long term you will be healthier. If you are in a state of extended stress or anxiety it is very difficult to maintain weight, and general health. The resulting physiology of the Sympathetic Nervous System is the exact opposite of that of the

Parasympathetic. The physiological results when the Sympathetic Nervous System is in control are:

Eye Pupils Dilate	Liver Releases Glucose
Inhibits Saliva Production	Kidneys Release Epinephrine & Norepinephrine
Increased Heart Rate	
	Relaxes the Bladder
Dilates Bronchi	
	Contracts the Rectum
Inhibits or Stops Peristalsis	
	Peripheral Vasoconstriction

However, the reptilian brain along with the limbic system, or mammalian brain (discussed in the next chapter) can also cause you to move subconsciously in response to threatening situations. Just as you can consciously manipulate some of the functions of the autonomic nervous system, the subconscious can manipulate movements that are commonly made consciously, such as lifting a finger, scratching your nose or wringing your hands. This "hijacking" of movements by the subconscious creates "Emotional Leaks", the importance of which we will discuss in a later chapter.

The Reptile Brain and Social Status

Additionally, the reptilian brain puts a great deal of importance on social status. The drive to be the "alpha" of the group is one of our primal drives. Many, however, deny this drive because of the emotions of the mammalian brain and will settle for lower social status. Status is also somewhat subjective based on the group with whom you associate. The "alpha" in a chess club, would not likely be the "alpha" in a mixed martial arts gym.

The reason social status is important to an unemotional part of the brain is because throughout history social hierarchy has served to determine mating rights, as well as all the other perks of being the alpha. In mating, as with most other functions in the group, the "alphas" are typically given first choice, which means the successful perpetuation of their genes for another generation, and likely to be alpha's, as well. Additionally, those of lower status are often cut off, or shunned from the group. Rejection or isolation from the "group" is worse than death to the reptile brain.

The easiest way to remember what drives the reptilian brain re the five "F's" – Freeze – Flight – Fight – Feed – Fornicate. This is the basis of all our primal drives. The primal drives are critically important to know and understand as you interact with others. The reptilian brain evaluates new stimuli based on whether it should freeze, and hope to be unnoticed by it, flee from it to get to safety, stand and fight it, eat it, or mate with it.

There has been a lot of material written about how to "control" or how to "get around" the "Reptile Brain", as though our primal drives are a bad thing. I would argue that your primal drives are your best friends. They instinctively protect you from potential attacks; keep you from starving, freezing, falling, getting hit by traffic, finding a mate and many other beneficial behaviors. It is, however, also true that the "Reptile Brain" can get us in trouble when unchecked by the other parts of the brain. For example, if you walk out into the street and suddenly you realize there is an oncoming car and the "Reptile" goes into Freeze mode rather than flee, you are going to get run over. The emotion of fear from the Limbic System or

"Mammalian Brain" (as we will look at later) may be required to flip the switch from freeze to flee.

The Four Things You Must Understand

It is in the knowledge of how the reptilian brain behaves that we gain true power over it. The reptilian brain cannot be changed in any way. However, by understanding its natural instinctively primitive behavior we can use its natural behavior to achieve the best outcome for all parties. I have listed four that I feel are the most important to understand about the amazingly powerful Reptile Brain.

The first thing you need to understand about this most primitive part of the brain is that its primary objective outside of your autonomic body functions is to protect you and make sure you survive both physically and genetically. In so doing the reptilian brain is always on the lookout for potential threats, food and mates.

The second and critical thing to understand about the reptilian brain is how it processes information. The reptilian brain does not understand language or words, it has no emotions, it has no capacity to understand right from wrong, it knows no logic or reason and it CANNOT lie. The reptilian brain only knows its prime directive, keep you safe, keep you alive, and make sure you leave offspring. That's it. However, the actions of the reptile brain can cause the "human brain" to attempt to become deceptive. If the reptile signals fear, the human (cognitive) brain may try to overcome the fear through deception.

The third aspect you need to understand is that while it is the smallest of the three parts of the brain and is only responsible for five primary functions outside the autonomic functions of the body, it is quite possibly the most influential of the three parts of the triune brain. Without the reptile brain, life could not exist, because it controls all the motor functions of the body. It also controls some involuntary muscle movements such as ducking, flinching, blocking, etc., that are typically conscious movements. In fact, when the reptile brain makes these movements, they are much quicker and likely to succeed than when done consciously.

Fourth and finally, because the reptile brain controls our primal drives, it is by far the most influential part of the brain in decision making. When we make decisions the first assessment made is whether we will be harmed by the decision. It is important here to understand that the Reptile Brain considers change and loss as a form of pain or threat. Our Reptile Brain prefers the known over the unknown. When something is known, even if it is socially, physically, or financially harmful to us the Reptile will hold on to what it knows. Therefore, it is often difficult for a sales professional to change the mind of a prospect, even when they have a product or service that is clearly superior to the one the prospect is currently using. The logical, analytical brain of the prospect is being overridden by their Reptile Brain. And when the Cognitive (Human) Brain, does battle with the Reptile Brain...the Reptile wins almost every time.

It is for that reason at the beginning of this chapter I listed the Reptile Brain as being the highest in importance in the decision-making hierarchy. This very small part of the brain has enormous power over our behavior. Because it acts only on primal drives and doesn't understand language, emotion, or logic, it can be a formidable opponent.

The Reptile Dance

If you have ever watched Martial Artists perform attack and defense drills, you will see what looks like a choreographed dance. And to a degree it is just that. This is important because it teaches muscle memory responses.

Each move is precise; the offensive move is countered in perfect timing consciously. However, when it comes to an actual fight; the successful fighter is the one who "thinks" the least. The one who lets the reptilian mind take control will always fare better than the fighter who relies on cognitive thought. The reptilian fighter doesn't consciously think about attacking or defending. In reality, they have almost no conscious thought whatsoever.

A reptilian fighter does not consciously look for openings nor do they consciously watch out for incoming attacks. It is all done at the reptilian level. By doing so the fighter becomes much faster, more accurate and harder to hit, because they are operating from a part of the mind that gathers and processes huge amounts of data and is nearly two times faster than the cognitive mind and its limited capacity to handle data.

Additionally, the reptilian fighter is emotionless. They are not angry or scared, they are simply performing the task of self-preservation using the skills they acquired through the training drills and moving them over from the conscious to subconscious action. Therefore, one of the easiest ways to defeat someone in a fight is to get them mad. When a fighter gets mad, he loses control and speed because he has moved his efforts from the subconscious mind back to the conscious.

We see the same dance when people lie. When someone says something consciously that violates a primal drive it awakens the reptile brain in that person, which is what the lie detector is looking for. Knowing this gives you a decided advantage over the liar.

Chapter Summary

In this chapter, you have learned about the smallest yet most powerful part of the human mind, the R-Complex or

Reptile Brain. The reptile brain is responsible for all our primal drives. It operates without being bothered by emotion, logic or reason. It has the specific purpose of keeping us alive and making certain that our genes are carried to the next generation. It is for these reasons that the reptile brain has no capacity for deception, although it can cause the highest part of the brain, the Neocortex, or, human brain to do so.

What violates the primal drives and core values of one person may not be the same in another. What creates comfort and safety in one person's mind may constitute threat, loss or discomfort in another. Something that causes terrible fear in one person may be quite comfortable to another.

In the next chapter, we are going to take a close look at how the mind makes powerful emotional attachments and associations which create the set of core values that reinforce the primal drives of the Reptile Brain. So, let's move on to the Limbic System, or the Mammalian Brain.

« Chapter 5 »
Your Emotional Brain

Scientific Name: Limbic System

Common Names – Limbic System / "Paleomammalian Brain"/ "Mammalian Brain"

Primary Functions – Emotions / Associations / Patterns

Decision Making Hierarchy – High

Capacity to Lie – None

Where is the Emotional Limbic System?

Just above the Reptilian Brain, in the mid-brain region is the area which makes up the Paleomammalian brain or the limbic system. For our purposes, we will simply call this part of the brain the "Mammalian Brain". All mammals have this part of the brain in varying sizes in proportion to body size of the animal. The human limbic system is proportionally larger than any other species with primates being a very close second.

The Mammalian Brain's primary function is storage and recall of emotional memories and experiences. Think of it as a computer hard drive. When you're born, the drive is formatted but for the most part empty. When you draw your first breath the drive starts to fill. It fills with memories and experiences assigning them positive, negative or neutral emotional charge. We are most impressionable when we are young because of the lack of reference material available to the mammalian brain. That is why most phobias form when we are young. Over time the brain builds in critical faculties through which information is allowed into or rejected from entering our subconscious mind. This typically occurs sometime between the ages of 5 to 8 years of age depending on the child. Before those faculties or filters are established, pretty much anything and everything we are exposed to goes straight into the subconscious mind and stays there for life.

As the emotional center of the mind, the limbic or mammalian brain is tremendously influential about what we do and like or won't or don't like. It stores and controls our emotions and associations and is largely responsible for storage and recall of long-term memories and their meanings, and interprets what brings us pleasure or pain, what makes us happy or sad, based on past experience and associations.

The Neural Network

Though I compared our subconscious mind to that of a computer hard drive there is one very distinct difference. A computer drive is binary. The files stored are a series of 1's and 0's in a specific pattern and are limited to the hard limits of the drive. Our subconscious is not binary. The mind is a complex system of neural networks. These networks are made up of simple and complex neural pathways. They are completely intertwined and virtually limitless in their capacity to store, organize and retrieve data. The neural pathways in your mind may be weak or strong depending on the frequency of use, and the power of the emotions present when they were established and reinforced. In a fraction of a second, traumatic or highly emotionally charged experiences can instantly create neural pathways that are nearly impossible to break. Other experiences take more time but are just as powerful. Immediately following the trauma of being born, most of us quickly feel the loving warmth of our mother's arms holding us safely and comfortably. We quickly create neural pathways associated with our mother's love. If we are honest about it, even as adults, when we feel insecure, sick or troubled we want our mother to comfort and reassure us.

The neural pathways, by association form into neural networks transferring the feelings associated with one experience to that of something or someone else. These networks come to define us as who we are. They are networks of cognitive learning, memory, associations, emotions, patterned behaviors, and triggers.

Every time we are exposed to new data, or stimuli, once passed by the reptile, our mammalian brain next goes into its vast storage system. As we experience events it is this part of the brain that builds neural networks associated with the events. These networks can be reinforced or deconstructed based on new and sometimes more powerful events. However, the more reinforcements these networks receive the more difficult they are to deconstruct. Additionally, the stronger the experience the stronger the reinforcement or neural pathway. For example, it may take only one extremely traumatic event to create a permanent neural pathway that will be forever associated with that event, recreating the trauma every time it is triggered.

Living in the Rut

The brain is considerably lazy. It doesn't like to think. Thinking requires a great deal of energy. Therefore, we spend most of our time remembering and associating rather than actually thinking. We form habits and patterns of behavior and continue through life comfortably strolling down the rut our behavioral patterns have created. We know from the previous chapter that the reptilian brain hates change, which fits quite nicely with the mammalian brain's avoidance to pain. Combined, this is a recipe for life that few can, or want to escape.

A practical example of this would be an animal path. If you have a dog, spent any time in the woods or have ever gone hiking you'll know exactly what I mean. A dog for example will tend to walk the same path in your yard creating a pathway. At first the pathway is almost unnoticeable. However, over time you will begin to see where the dog walks, then one day you will notice that you have a dirt pathway to the extent that a rut has formed in your yard. The same is true in the woods. Deer, foxes, rabbits, and even humans will tend to make distinctive pathways through the woods that are easily noticeable. Your brain works in much the same way when forming neural pathways.

These networks or neural pathways once formed are nearly impossible to change no matter how irrational they may be. There are those who are terrified of escalators, elevators, stairways, spiders, ladders, etc., none of which pose a real threat to them, yet even the thought of the things can send them into a panic.

The same can work with pleasure. A person can experience an extremely pleasurable event one time, and from that time forward they associate that item or event with extreme pleasure. A person can use crystal meth one time and become an addict for life because the intensity and pleasure they experience is so strong they don't consider the downside of the addiction.

Thoughts, Emotions and Behavioral Patterns

The emotional brain does not function only in the extreme. When someone asks you if you'd like to go out to eat, you most likely get an instant list of places you'd like to go in a hierarchical order based on the pleasure you gain from each. You may first think of steak, then pizza, followed by sushi and finally barbeque. If the other person suggests seafood, you may agree, but it may be much further down on your list of favorites, or you may have gotten very sick on seafood one time and express your desire to eat somewhere else.

Once these patterns of behavior are established the trained eye can notice them. Not only can they notice them, they can see the degree to which they are used, the frequency the path is accessed and recognize the triggers that put the person on that pathway. This is one way that sales professionals, negotiators, psychologists, psychiatrists, marketers and many others can easily manipulate others. If you know the triggers that cause a certain behavior you can quickly and easily evoke the emotional response necessary to get that person in the desired state be it positive or negative and to have that person behave with a very predictable behavior.

Pleasure vs. Pain

Humans operate in one of two primary ways when it comes to pain and pleasure. We either move away from pain then toward pleasure, or toward pleasure then away from pain. Although they sound almost the same, they are vastly different. Most of us are the Pain / Pleasure rather than Pleasure / Pain. Marketing professionals are perhaps the number one users of this science. They understand that human nature in the vast majority of people is to do two things. We naturally move away from pain/loss then we move toward pleasure/gain. Marketing messages are largely formed around the principle of pain avoidance first and pleasure secondarily. Even ads for elaborate tropical vacations will often mention the pain of the potential vacationer before going into the pleasures of going.

Most successful advertising has little to do with logic, reason, or rational thinking and everything to do with emotions, the avoidance of pain and the gain of pleasure. When done effectively the logical "human" brain, the Neocortex is only engaged after the fact to rationalize and justify the decision made by the emotional "mammalian" brain. Television, by the way has made this much easier because television is visual, which is the primary way most of us learn. Then add persuasion and influence language and you have the makings of a highly effective ad.

State Control

The mammalian brain is also responsible for your mental "state". It determines your mood. If you are happy, it is because your mammalian brain has put you in that state. If you are sad, mad, etc. it is the emotional mammalian brain that set that mood. Many people believe that you cannot simply decide to change your mental state, when in fact they simply don't want it to change. We get "stuck" in an emotional state and rather than do something about it we tend to just stay there.

If you are going to successfully detect lies, you must become a master of state control. Changing state can be as simple as a decision. Sometimes it may require more than a decision. Find emotional anchors that tie you to the state of mind you wish to experience. We all have both positive and negative anchors set in our minds. Anchors are much like a trigger that cause our minds to go to a specific place, time or state. An anchor can be a specific type of touch, sound, smell, taste or image that causes an instant psychological response. There may be a smell such as the smell of cooking yeast rolls that instantly takes you to a place or time that you remember your mother or grandmother cooking, or the smell of your favorite cookies baking in the oven, a song that takes you back to a favorite memory in the past, a specific way that your mother used to touch you to console you when you were upset. It could be any number of things. It is very important to know that anchors exist and that they are powerful. It is also important to note that new anchors can quickly and easily be set. Someone who is skilled at NLP (neuro linguistic programming) can set anchors in a variety of ways with or without a person's knowledge in order to elicit and control another person's state. Even a person who has no knowledge of NLP can set an anchor in another person without realizing it which is extremely dangerous and can be very harmful to the person who has the anchor set.

The one other vitally important thing to understand about the Mammalian brain is that it is here where our values, ethics, morals and beliefs are stored. They work in conjunction with and are interpretations of our primal drives, but even so, they can still be trumped by the Reptile. Let's say, for example you are a young man or woman who doesn't believe in sex before marriage. However, you suddenly find yourself in a situation of great "temptation". You may be far from home, where no one would find out. You may find yourself particularly attracted to someone, a person who is particularly attracted to you. Something happens and suddenly you find yourself completely overwhelmed by a "primal urge" that you just cannot seem to control. The "Reptile" makes the decision to override your morals. This decision is then fed to your "Human Brain" (which we'll cover later), where it is rationalized and justified. It happens all the time. This is the Power of the "Reptile Brain".

However, the emotional "Mammalian Brain", along with the logical "Human Brain", can somewhat maintain control keeping one's morals intact by preempting the "Reptile's" Primal Drives. By simply keeping the person away from tempting situations that would allow the "Reptile" that opportunity. Therefore, a person who gets great pleasure from drinking should avoid finding themselves in a bar at all cost. They simply cannot overcome the power of the "Reptile's" desire.

The final attribute of the "Mammalian Brain" is the fact that it has no capacity to lie. This part of the mind functions on real feelings and raw emotion. It has no capacity to manufacture falsehood or deception. It can, however, be deceived into believing inaccurate information. For instance, it can become convinced that all dogs bite, a specific race is dishonest or subhuman, and truly believe the lie. In these cases, when the person states that "all dogs bite", even though the statement is untrue, it is not a lie to the person making the statement and no hot spots will appear.

Chapter Summary

The takeaway from this chapter is that the emotional core values, ethics, and beliefs of the "Mammalian Brain", reinforce and supercharge the power of the "Reptile Brain" in decision making. The "Mammalian" and "Reptilian Brains" make up the subconscious mind and together they are a nearly unstoppable force in decision making. In fact, scientists estimate that the subconscious mind is responsible for approximately 96% to 98% of all decisions made.

The true power of deception analysis lies in the ability to recognize the messages being sent as the result of a person's subconscious core beliefs and values held in the "Mammalian" and "Reptilian" brains being in conflict with the "Human" brain, which we will cover next. If you can, you are well on your way to becoming a human lie detector.

« Chapter 6 »
Your Human Brain

Scientific Name: Neocortex

Common Names – "Neomammalian Brain" / "Human Brain"

Primary Functions – Logic / Analysis / Language / Critical Thinking

Decision Making Function – Low

Capacity to Lie – High

Where is the Logical, Rational Neocortex?

The wrinkled outer part of the brain is called the Neocortex or the Neomammalian Brain. The Neocortex is the last part of the brain to form. The Neocortex is also divided into two halves which are connected by a network of nerves called the Corpus Callosum. This part of the brain, while found in many animals is, as a percentage of brain to body weight greatest in humans. Therefore, we will refer also refer to the Neocortex as the "human" brain.

What does the Neocortex do?

The Neocortex, or the "human" brain is responsible for many functions, but for our purpose we will be focusing on its purpose of handling cognition. The Neocortex or human brain, and primarily the pre-frontal lobes of the Neocortex are most notably responsible for critical analysis, language and problem solving. It in effect handles our executive or higher thinking processes. It is also commonly referred to as our conscious mind, while the Limbic System and R-Complex make up the Subconscious mind.

Firstly, the conscious mind is comparatively slow in comparison to the other two parts of the brain. The subconscious mind functions at approximately 1.5 times faster than the conscious or cognitive mind. This means that we respond to stimuli at a level below consciousness long before our conscious mind even recognizes the stimulus exists. Although this occurs in a fraction of a second, it is very significant.

Secondly, while very powerful, it is also somewhat limited in its capacity. The human brain is particularly limited in its ability to process multiple streams of input or stimuli. It is estimated that most people can only consciously track five to seven bits, or chunks of information at one time, plus or minus two. If we attempt to track too many things simultaneously, we go into a condition known as cognitive overload at which point the cognitive brain becomes overwhelmed and "shuts down".

The "bits" or "chunks" of information can vary in size and complexity as your cognitive brain tries to build associations in order to cram as much information into one "chunk" of information as it can. When you look at a car you do not see it as each component part beginning with the lug nuts. You simply see a car. Your cognitive mind cannot process all the parts individually; therefore it "chunks" all the components up into one understandable unit. At that point it can begin to break, or "chunk" the car down into smaller units such as the powertrain, the interior, the body style, etc.

Have you ever wondered why the dashes were placed in phone numbers, Social Security numbers and most other important numbers you need to remember, and why they are typically broken into 3 to 4 digits between dashes? It is for this very reason. Look at the number below for a few seconds then look away and see if you remember it...

18126776298

Odds are you had a difficult time remembering this number. There are simply too many bits of information for your cognitive brain to handle because you made each digit a chunk of information. However, if you were to look at the number like this...

1-812-677-6298

The number is now much easier to handle. You have only four "chunks" or "bits" of information to process, each of which contain four or less digits. We learn to spell the same way. The word Mississippi for example. You most likely learned it as "Miss-iss-ippi", or Albuquerque, "Albu-quer-que". Each containing three sets of no more than four letters allowing the cognitive mind to process, understand in a way in which it could recall it from long-term memory. Nursery rhymes, poems, even the Pledge of Allegiance are broken down this way.

It is the limitations of the Neocortex, or, human brain that makes deception analysis possible. The conscious mind can only track 5 to 7 +/-2 bits of information. The subconscious mind can track millions. These facts, coupled with its overwhelming speed advantage of the subconscious means that while we may consciously try to conceal the truth, the subconscious beats the conscious to the punch and reveals the truth before the conscious mind can hide it.

The Lying Brain

The "human" brain is the only part of the mind capable of dishonesty. Because of its ability to reason it may determine a situation to be best suited with deception. While the emotional limbic system may understand the pain associated with telling the truth, it cannot lie. Therefore, the conscious (human) brain makes up a falsehood to avoid the pain of the truth. Unfortunately, the pain that results from lying may ultimately be greater than the truth had it been told.

Since the two primitive parts of the brain are much faster and have exponentially more capacity to handle input than the newer part, and they have no capacity for deception, the truth always leaks out if you know what to look for.

Chapter Summary

In this chapter we looked at the human part of the brain, the Neocortex. You discovered that the conscious mind is incredibly powerful but limited in its ability to process and track only a fraction of the input it receives while the subconscious is much faster and has a nearly limitless ability to process and track input.

You also learned that the conscious mind, or the "human" brain, is the only part of the mind that is capable of deception and it is for this reason the truth will always come out. It may be very subtle, and typically is, but it will come out

Introduction to Deception Analysis

« Chapter 7 »
Deception Analysis

The Truth About Catching Lies

Many people don't believe it's possible to accurately detect when a person is lying. However, that is untrue. A person can, with a great degree of accuracy, recognize when a person is being deceptive.

A common misconception in being able to spot lies is that we are looking for the lie as a "gotcha" type of thing. Nothing could be further from the truth. In reality detecting deception is about finding the truth, not catching a lie. Even in criminal interrogations, the objective is to find the truth. We already know they're going to lie.

We all lie, we lie a lot and we do it very badly. Most untrained people will miss as many as 80% of the 8-200 lies, we're told each day. Even so, most think they're pretty good at spotting the lies they're told.

I've had countless people tell me, "I've been in this business for, how ever many years and I always know when someone's lying to me". Unfortunately, the truth is, even if they are looking for deception, they'll only catch about 54%. Basically, it's a toss of a coin whether or not they'll catch a lie. Even those in law enforcement, judges and attorneys, whose job it is to get to the truth are only slightly better than the average person on the street, unless they've been specifically trained to do so.

Once trained, the ability to spot lies is a powerful skill to possess. It is, however, a two-edged sword. While it's fun to have the skill, once you know what to look for you will begin to understand the amazing frequency of the lies you hear every day. Not just from strangers but from close family and friends. The average person lies nearly three times per ten minutes of conversation. How many people do you talk to in a day?

In the beginning it can be frustrating, but as you get into it more you realize that while you're being lied to a lot, most of it just doesn't matter. I hear dozens of lies each day and while I may notice them, I choose to do nothing with them. Even if I do respond to a lie, the liar will most likely not know they've been caught. I simply redirect them, in order to find the truth. On occasion I will call someone out, but it's very rare in my line of work.

The information in this book will in no way make you a skilled deception analyst. It will, however, give you a working knowledge of how to spot the majority of the lies you're told if you practice. If you're the only person in your office to read this and can increase your ability to spot lies by just 15% you would be miles ahead of everyone else.

Just imagine what this skill would do for you if you're in Management, HR or sales. Imagine being able to spot the lies that nearly 60% of people tell in their Resume'/CV. Or being able to tell when your employees are lying to you. What about having the ability to know, when negotiating a deal, when and how the other person is lying (100% of all business deals involve deception). Or maybe you're an employee looking for a raise. Wouldn't it be advantageous to know when and if your boss is lying to you? What if you suspect your spouse or significant other is cheating on you? Wouldn't it be valuable to instantly, automatically see when they're lying? Obviously, it is always beneficial to be able to accurately detect lies.

There are three primary ways to catch a liar:

1. Lying by Comparison – Having a person lie on a control question. Once you see someone lie, they will typically lie the same way on future relevant questions

2. Verbal indicators of deception – When a person lies, often their language will reveal their deception. What they say, what they DON'T say, and the way they say it often betrays the liar.

3. Physical indications of deception – Just as our words can betray us, so too can our body. When a person lies it is done consciously. The subconscious cannot lie and therefore we can see this in the body movements of the liar.

Chapter Summary

In this chapter you discovered that "human lie detection" is actually based in science. You learned that the ability to detect deception is real and reliable.

You were introduced to the three ways to catch a liar. We'll be taking a closer look at each of the three ways in which people lie to us for much of the remainder of the book.

« Chapter 8 »
Nonverbal Communication

The Body Speaks

Far beyond our spoken words the body speaks out. Regardless of how hard we might try we cannot keep the body from telling the truth. If what you are saying is incongruent with your true feelings or is untrue your body leaks out clues that signal the trained eye to know something is wrong about what you're saying.

As with all Hot Spots, one body signal is not enough to know for certain someone is lying. The exception would be micro expressions which are a leaking of true emotion. So, for example, you tell me you're happy about something and during your statement your eyebrows pull up and together (sadness), I know you're lying. Micro expressions flash across the face in less than half a second and it requires extensive training to detect them accurately. It is for that reason we will not be going in depth on micro expressions in this book.

You will also see subtle expressions which last between one half to one second. These are a little easier to detect. And then there are macro expressions which last more than a second and can be manipulated to some degree, while others are nearly impossible to manipulate even when we try. For example, a true smile is very difficult to fake. When we display a genuine smile not only do the corners of the lips turn up, but wrinkles form on the outside of the eyes caused by the flexing of the orbicularis oculi muscles surrounding the eyes. Very few people (less than 10%) can consciously flex these muscles.

Two or more hot spots when seen/heard together create a "cluster". This is what's needed in order truly detect a lie.

It's not what you say, but how you say it

There is much more in what a person may say than just the words. We'll look at some of the specific Hot Spots that deal with word analysis in a later chapter. Right now, we are focusing on the way a person uses their voice nonverbally. When a person deviates their speech patterns in response to a relevant question, this is a Hot Spot.

Generally, when we speak, we use the same tone and timbre; we speak at pretty much the same pitch and pace, as well. These speech patterns are obviously contextual. A person, when sad, will not use the same pattern as when they're happy.

However, when faced with a relevant question one could change their pattern. This is especially important to note when a person's speech pattern deviates from what you would normally expect. If, for example, a person was to tell you they were happy about something, but frown and speak in a low, slow monotone voice, there's something wrong. That's a hot spot. That person is most likely NOT happy.

Chapter Summary

In this chapter we discussed the fact that much more information flows nonverbally between people in a one-on-one conversation than do our words.

We discussed looking for specific Hot Spots that have been proven to have a high degree of accuracy in detecting lies. And we now know that one Hot Spot is never enough to prove deception. A cluster of two or more are necessary to determine if someone is lying.

When looking for deception the first and most important thing is to look for ANY behavior in body or speech that departs from that person's baseline body and speech patterns. It could be as simple as twitching a finger, clearing the throat or changing pitch, pace, volume or wording the person is using.

Hot Spots

« Chapter 9 »
Lying by Comparison

What is Lying by Comparison?

The first type of deception analysis we're going to look at is the comparison method. While this is the most accurate method to spotting lies, it is probably the least useful for anyone who is not conducting interviews or interrogations.

The comparison method takes baselining to a higher level. In most baselining methods the interviewer is establishing how a person behaves under normal, relaxed conditions and in casual conversation.

The comparison method takes this one step further. In the comparison method we establish not only the subject's behavior in casual conversation, but also baseline what that person does when lying.

This is accomplished by asking the subject three types of questions. They are:

- Relaxed Casual Questions – Baselining normal behavior by asking questions to which the person would have no reason to lie.

- Control Questions – Questions in which we expect someone lie in order to establish a deceptive behavioral baseline.

- Relevant questions – Questions that are relevant to the interview's objectives.

The Process

In this type of interview, the interviewer will start with non-threatening casual conversation and questions to put the interviewee at ease and to see how the person behaves when telling the truth. The interviewer notes how the person behaves with this type of questions.

The interviewer will then ask a control question. This type of question is something the interviewer would expect the interviewee to lie about. Questions such as, "Did you give 100% at your last job?", "Are you always honest?", or "Have you ever been tempted to steal something from work?" We know everyone is guilty of each of these questions, or most of them anyway.

The interviewer will ask one control question and note what the person does differently and how they answer. Did they move a hand, move their head or a foot, did they change their speech patterns or voice? Whatever the person does that varies from the established relaxed baseline is noted.

After the control question is asked the interviewer goes back to casual conversation and questions to allow the interviewee to return to a normal state. This pattern of casual and control questioning is completed three or four times. Each time the interviewee answers a control question the interviewer notes any changes in behavior or language.

At that point the interviewer has, not only a baseline for normal relaxed behavior, but also has a baseline for their deceptive behavior as well. Each time, allowing the interviewee to return to a normal state.

It's important to mention again that everyone lies differently, but most individuals will lie the same way. By using the control questions, the interviewer knows exactly what the interviewee does when lying. These behaviors will only be magnified or added to when faced with a relevant question.

At this point the interviewer is ready to ask the relevant questions. These questions are the ones that actually matter to the interviewer. The interviewer will allow the person to get in a relaxed nondeceptive state then ask a relevant question and notice what the person does. If their behavioral response is the same as in a control question, the interviewer knows the response was a lie. The interviewer will still look for other Hot Spots to the relevant questions as well and document them.

Once again after answering the relevant question the interviewer will bring the interviewee back to a relaxed non-deceptive state by asking returning to casual conversation and nonrelevant questions. This process is completed until all the relevant questions have been answered.

Chapter Summary

In this chapter you learned that this is by far the most accurate means by which to detect deception. You learned the basics of conducting an interview using casual, control and relevant questions.

Unfortunately, most of us do not have the luxury of a formal interview when detecting deception. Most of our detection is in normal conversation, watching a presentation, etc.

For that we need the skills that are taught in the next two chapters.

« Chapter 10 »
Verbal Indications of Deception

What are Verbal Hot Spots?

When we speak, we speak in certain ways depending on context. We have a common pace, pitch and pattern in our normal speech. Whenever faced with a relevant question, a person's voice or speech patterns change which is a red flag for the deception analyst to pay closer attention to.

It is important to make sure you can get a baseline of the person's behavior while relaxed. Next, it's good if you can, watch the person lie to control questions. Control questions are questions to which we expect the person to lie.

An example of a control question that might come up in a job interview would be, "Did you always give 100% at your previous place of employment?" We know that no one gives 100% to anything, but the unsuspecting job applicant will likely answer in the affirmative in order to protect himself.

When questioned, you may notice the person answers almost immediately rather than their normal response rate to other questions. You may notice they change the words they use or a host of other variations to their speech.

In this chapter we're going to look at some of the most commonly used and most accurate verbal Hot Spots. While these indicators are highly indicative of a lie by themselves, they are not 100%. Therefore, you should look for two or more in order to prove the person is lying.

Also keep in mind that people from other cultures can and do make mistakes with their language. Additionally, grammar in some countries is different than ours. If you are speaking to a person whose first language is not English you will need to eliminate some of the verbal indicators, as this book is written for grammar common to English.

I have placed the indicators in a way that allows you room on the page to make notes, jot down scenarios that are contextually correct for your situation.

Verbal Hot Spots

1. Removing Contractions

When we speak, we typically use a lot of contractions. It is, however, important to note how a subject uses them. Some academics and in the professions naturally speak in very emphatic language, so they don't use nearly as many contractions as you or I do.

When faced with a relevant question, people will often drop their contractions and go into emphatic language. This is a very common and highly accurate Hot Spot.

An example would be:

Question: Did you take my pen?

Answer: I did not take your pen?

An honest answer would be something such as, "No", or "No, I didn't take your pen".

Once you begin to look for this Hot Spot, you'll see it used a lot and is very accurate.

2. Distancing Language

When a person suddenly stops using personal pronouns and specific names, we refer to it as "Distancing Language". The liar wants to put space between themselves and the lie.

When we speak, we typically take ownership of what we're saying. Often a liar will "distance" themselves from the lie by removing the pronouns or specific names in response to a relevant question.

This, too, is a very common and highly accurate Hot Spot.

An example would be:

Question: Did you take my pen?

Answer: I would never do that.

An honest answer would be something such as, "No", or "No, I didn't take your pen".

This one sounds a little weird to us, but makes perfect sense to the liar. Most of the hot spots in this book are the result of an unconscious process.

3. Speaks too quickly – rehearsed story

With this indicator the liar starts talking almost before the question is complete. When people are given time, they will fabricate a story. Not knowing exactly what the questions will be, the story may contain details of things not asked about.

Example:

Question: Why were you late for work?

Answer: (starts the instant the question is complete) "I started for work this morning after I had my bacon and eggs for breakfast. On the way here I noticed the time on the bank clock, which said I had plenty of time. I got behind a white lawn care company van that was going very slowly. When I got here, I saw Joe out in the parking lot, he was smoking a cigarette, and I talked to him for a minute.

4. Deflections

This is a very common Hot Spot. It is a liar's favorite because it sounds to the untrained ear as though the question has been answered, when in fact, it has not.

Generally, when asked a question we give a direct answer. Often times when a person is lying their answer will shift to an indirect answer.

This, too, is highly accurate Hot Spot.

An example would be:

Question: Did you take my pen?

Answer: Why would I take your pen; I have a perfectly good one.

As I said, to the untrained ear there doesn't appear to be anything wrong with this answer. It sounds as though the person has answered honestly when in fact there is a very high probability the person is lying.

5. Using humor when asked a serious question

Often times the liar will respond inappropriately to a serious question or when making a serious point. You will see someone laugh while lying in response to a relevant question.

Not long ago a celebrity filed a claim that someone had beaten him up in a racist attack. While recalling the story in what would normally be a painful statement, the celebrity laughed while recalling a part of the alleged incident. When you're describing being attacked you don't laugh. Some would say the person was trying to laugh off the pain. In this case, however, the inappropriate laughing was used on numerous occasions and in conjunction with other Hot Spots. We give everyone the presumption of innocence; however, as a deception analyst my opinion is that he was covering the truth about the incident in multiple points in his interview.

6. *Restating a question as a negative statement*

In this indicator the liar is searching for the quickest easiest way to answer the question.

In order to try to cover their lie, the liar takes a linguistic shortcut, thinking they are answering the question in a way that will cover their guilt.

Untrained listeners will often take the bait and believe the liar.

Examples:

Question: Did you take the pen?

Answer: No, I did not take the pen.

Question: Did you call on his client?

Answer: No, I have no reason to call on his client.

7. Convincers

Very often when a person lies, they feel compelled to add mild oaths or other additional language in order to convince the person to whom they are speaking that they are telling the truth. People often fall for this indicator because it sounds like the person is reinforcing their innocence when, in fact, they are confessing to their guilt.

Some examples of convincing language include, but are not limited to:

- Swear to God
- To tell you the truth
- Honestly
- I have no reason to lie
- I'm only going to say this once

8. Stalling

Another very accurate indicator is stalling. Stalling occurs when the liar needs to stop and think up their lie. If the question is not one that would generally require one to think about an answer, such as, "What did you have for lunch last Wednesday"? When recall or calculation, etc. are not required a person should answer in about one second. If that person delays two or more seconds to a relevant question, but doesn't normally, there's a high probability they're lying.

9. Qualifiers or, Qualifying Statements

Qualifying statements are also very accurate on their own, as well. When we lie, we often use qualifying statements to emphasize our innocence. When, in fact, to the trained listener we know the opposite to be true.

When you hear the examples below in response to a relevant question there's a very high probability the person has lied.

- That's an excellent question.
- Could you be more specific?
- It's not as simple as yes or no.
- Could you repeat the question?
- It depends on what you mean.
- How dare you ask me that!
- Where did you hear that?

10. Jumping between present to past tense

Often when a person is giving an account by telling a story that involves deception, you'll hear that person jump back and forth between present and past tense.

The story should be recalled from memory, which means it should be set in the past. However, the liar is creating all or part of the story, which means to the subconscious mind the story is happening in real time, or in the present.

An example of this would be:

Question: "Why were you late getting back from lunch?"

Answer: Well, after I finished lunch I started back to the office. Then there's an accident that has traffic backed up for over a mile. Once I got through the traffic I came straight back to the office and I'm 15 minutes late getting here.

In this example the liar jumps from present to past tense two different times. While there may be some truth in the statement, there was most likely no accident, or if there was it didn't slow the person down that badly, and it is likely that the person was actually more than 15 minutes late getting back.

11. Improper introduction of articles

Once again improperly introducing articles into a story is a common practice when lying.

An "article" or object should be introduced into a story using words like "a_____", "an_____", "some_____", etc. Referring to an article as "the_____" first in a story is a Hot Spot.

Example:

Truth – "At first, I thought I saw your pen laying on the conference room table, but when I checked it was one of the company pens."

Lie – "Yesterday I noticed the car in front of the house; I didn't recognize it."

In the firsts example the person answers by introducing the article, "a pen" correctly.

In the second example the article "the car" is introduced incorrectly. Once again, since the story is being made up, the subconscious mind causes the person to introduce the article incorrectly, because in their mind the car had already been introduced into the story.

12. Exclusion words not used in a narrative

Liars tend to not say things they didn't do. They generally will only say what they did.

Listen for exclusion words in response to a relevant question or event.

Some exclusion words would include

- But
- Except
- Without
- Didn't
- Wouldn't
- Couldn't

And many more

An example would be:

Truth: I saw a pile of papers on the conference table. I was going to check and see what they were, but I didn't have time. When I came back, they were gone. I didn't realize they were your missing paperwork.

Lie: I noticed the pile of paperwork on the conference room table. I had an appointment coming in. When I came back, they were gone.

13. Text Bridging

A text bridge is often used to skip over parts of the story the liar wants to leave out rather than tell an outright lie.

Phrases often used as bridges include:

Finally

Afterwards

Besides

I don't remember

Later on

While

Before

The next thing I knew

Shortly thereafter

Even though

After that

When

Then

Consequently

However.

Example:

Earlier I went to lunch, ***after that*** I went to my doctor's appointment, ***shortly thereafter***, I returned to work. ***After that*** I went home. ***Later*** that evening I started on the project ***even though*** it was very late.

14. Speaking in muddled sentences

Often when formulating a story, the narrative in the conscious mind doesn't come out properly. Remember this is coming out in real time.

As the liar tells the story they may leave things out, may false start or restart a statement, or leave parts of the story out. It sounds strange to the listener, but make perfect sense to the liar.

Example

Umm... we headed out for the .... Conference.... you know, the expo. We had to hurry to get... only took the company van... Then we had to stop.... I mean, we finally made it... to, you know, the... umm...but the event had already started.

People actually do this more often than you've most likely noticed in the past, but you will see it more now that I've called it to your attention.

15. Sequence of a story

When telling the truth, a person may get the chronology wrong. It may not be in logical sequence. Probably because there is emotional attachment to our memories, but there is none in a made-up story.

When lying, the story will be in strict chronological order. Unfortunately for the liar, they typically only rehearse the story from first to last.

Many times, the liar cannot tell the story backwards, while a person recalling memory can typically do so.

This indicator is getting pretty low on the probability of indicating deception on its own. Be sure to have two or three additional indicators before accusing someone of lying.

Chapter Summary

In this chapter you've learned fourteen of the most common ways people lie with their words. There are many, many more ways people use words to lie, but these fourteen are among the most common.

« Chapter 11 »
Physical Indicators of Deception

When watching for physical Hot Spots it is again important to watch the person in a relaxed state with little or no signs of stress.

When a person is relaxed you will see things such as:

- Steepled hands

- Slight head tilt (too much tilt is a sign of flirting)

- Smooth flowing gestures

- No comforting gestures such as rubbing hands, or adjusting their clothing

- Not covering parts of their body as to hide something. Crossed arms, hand covering part of the face, etc.

Most Hot Spots are also indicators of stress. But, not all indicators of stress are indications of deception.

It is helpful to be able to baseline the individual's behavior on both casual and control questions. If you cannot, you must rely on "clusters". A cluster is when two or more hot spots are detected.

With verbal indicators we were looking for incongruence of the words a person uses. Likewise, with physical indicators we are looking for incongruence between the verbal message and what the body is doing.

There's nothing wrong with a person nodding their head "yes", unless they are saying "no" with their words. That would be a physical Hot Spot and should be noted. Watch and listen for other verbal or physical indicators, as well, in order to establish a cluster.

In most cases when someone lies, they will subconsciously "leak" the truth. The leak may come in the form of Verbal Expression, Physical Expression or both. The liar is NOT typically conscious of the leaks. When they do recognize they leaked something, it is usually after the fact.

Leakages are the same thing as Hot Spots.

What do we look for when detecting lies?

1. Train yourself to look at the face while remaining aware, through peripheral viewing, of the rest of the body. This takes practice and patience, but as you continue to practice you will find that you can look at both the face and the rest of someone's body simultaneously.

2. Listen carefully to what is said, and what is NOT said (Verbal Expression) while looking for physical Hot Spots that contradict their Verbal Expressions

For example, while looking at a someone's face you hear the subject answer 'yes', but you notice that they shook their head back and forth, indicating 'no'. You have just detected an indication of deception.

The physical indicators, like the verbal indicators, are only relevant when a person is confronted with a relevant question. That question may be asked or implied.

Any time the liar feels the consequences of the truth are worth the risk of a lie, you will often see these indicators as a result.

Physical Hot Spots

1. Emblematic Gestures in Detecting Deception

Emblematic Gestures are gestures that have global understanding within a specific culture. It is important to understand that not all emblematic gestures are the same in cultures outside of our own. For this reason, if you are traveling abroad it is helpful to know what the emblematic gestures are in that culture.

Emblems are gestures that need no verbal explanation in order to understand their meaning. We know, for example that nodding the head up and down is the emblem for agreement or "yes". No one needs to ask what someone means when nodding their head. It is emblematic.

Others that are common in our culture are, the middle finger, shrugging the shoulders, the "OK" hand gesture to name a few.

Emblematic gestures are the most accurate of all Hot Spots other than micro expressions, which we will cover separately in this book.

Emblematic gestures are the most accurate of all Hot Spots. When seen by themselves, emblems are over 90% indicative of deception. Not 100% but very close. Unless you're interviewing someone where you have watched the subject answer control questions (a question to which you expect a person answer with a lie) and watched that person lie, you still will need at least one other Hot Spot, either verbal or physical to be 100% certain they have lied.

Additionally, emblematic gestures are the only Hot Spots that are not stress induced. Emblems are more about emotion than stress, which is why they're so accurate.

Emblematic Gestures

Following is a list of emblematic gestures you should be looking for.

- Middle finger leakage

- Finger to the lips (self-hushing)

- Half or small shoulder shrugs (lack of confidence in what was said)

- Hand or Foot Shrug (lack of confidence, same as a shoulder shrug)

- Inconsistent head nodding

- Covering or touching the eyes (shame or sadness). Note: *Vigorous eye rubbing is not deceptive.*

- Looking down and away (guilt or shame)

- Thumbs up/Thumbs down

- Hiding hands (hiding the truth)

- Hand stop sign

- Facing palms downward or gesturing with the back of one's hand(s)

- Backing up – stepping, leaning or moving the head or body back after a statement (distancing)

- Placing objects between the other person and you (creates a subconscious barrier or wall)

2. Inconsistent Gestures or Expressions

Gestures should always be consistent with the words we speak. Whenever a person says one thing but their body/gestures display something else it's a hot spot and should be noted.

- Gesture or expression comes AFTER a statement is made.

    o Most expressions and gestures start slightly before the person begins speaking. When a gesture or expression occurs after a statement is made, it's a good sign of deception.

- Eyelids closed or half closed longer than a normal blink.

    o A normal blink occurs in a fraction of a second. If the person closes, or partially closes their eyes for a second or longer it is an indication of disagreement or deception.

- Asymmetrical Facial Gestures

    o Facial expressions should be symmetrical with the exception of contempt (in contempt only one side of the lip goes up). If only half of the face changes, such as in fake smile or when smiling while the eyes are displaying anger. (We'll discuss specifics about facial expressions and what emotions they demonstrate in a later chapter.)

- Facial expression doesn't match the statement

    o For example, a person smiles or laughs while verbally expressing another emotion such as sadness or anger

- Chin is scrunched or thrust forward and up

    o This is a sign of contempt or concealed anger

- Fake surprise

    o Eyebrows move up for more than 1 second.

        ▪ When a person is genuinely surprised the eyebrows are rounded and lifted up. If the person displays this expression for more than a second, they are faking surprise.

    o When a person answers a question with a question while showing surprise, they already know the answer to their own question.

- Sudden giggling for no reason, when they should be experiencing another emotion such as sadness or anger.

- Sudden lack of gestures to emphasize important points. Often when a person lies they will stop making their normal hand or body gestures. It's as important to watch for what doesn't happen as it is what does.

- Hands chopping out of sync with the points being emphasized.

- Shoulder shrug with one or both hands extended with palms up, in conjunction with a phrase such as, "I've told you the truth"

- The person is calm when they should be upset. Once again, it's what's not there that's important.

3. Disagreement Hot Spots or Gestures

This is another form of inconsistent gestures. These, however, show disagreement with their statement or the statement you make.

- Squinting eyes

- Lips compressed or pursed shows anger

- Lips sucked into the mouth, hiding or stopping from saying something

- One sided smile or smirk shows contempt

- Rolling of the eyes, out of context shows contempt

- Nose crinkled, pulling upper lip up, and possibly squinting eyes shows disgust

- Tone of voice flat or overly controlled. Voice volume gets lower shows lack of confidence in what they are saying

- Speech rate slows down shows a lack of confidence in what they are saying

4. Fight, Flight, Freeze Expressions or Gestures

When we go into a state of fight, flight, freeze the lowest part of the brain (the reptile brain) takes over and the autonomic nervous system changes from parasympathetic to sympathetic. When this occurs, our physiology can change rather dramatically, but are missed by most people who are untrained.

Some of these indicators can be hard to see, but they're very accurate if you can.

- Increased licking of the lips
    - In this state the mouth will almost instantly go dry as the fluid in the mouth is moved into the core and large smooth muscle groups.

- Voice cracking
    - In addition to licking the lips, because all the saliva has left the mouth the person's voice may crack or become raspy.

- Increased or frequently clearing the throat
    - Another side effect of having no saliva leaving the mouth and throat.

- Voice pitch goes higher in a sentence or a particular word.

- Pupils dilate
    - When in fight flight the pupils will change. If the person is afraid or aroused the pupils will dilate. If they are angry or preparing to

fight the pupils will narrow or get small. The pupil serves much like the aperture on a camera. It opens, in fear or arousal, to allow as much information in as possible. It closes and narrows the field of vision in order to "target stare" in preparation to strike.

- Facial muscles such as the lips, chin or cheeks tremble or twitch

- Voice trembling

- Increased blinking

- Difficulty swallowing or swallowing repeatedly

- Hands go cold

    o Once again as the state of fight, flight occurs and the nervous system switches from parasympathetic to sympathetic, blood is moved from the extremities into the core and large smooth muscle groups in the legs in preparation to fight or flee, leaving the hands colder than normal

- Fixed Eye Gaze – "Deer in the headlight".

    o It is often, but wrongly thought that a person won't look you in the eye when they lie. In fact, the exact opposite is true. A liar will often lock eyes with the person to whom they are lying. They need to make sure the person is buying their lie.

- Hands or posture become motionless as if frozen

    o Typically accompanied by the "deer in the headlight" look

- Sudden change in posture

    o Any time someone changes their posture in response to a relevant question it is a red flag regardless of what that posture may be.

- Rocking or fidgeting

    o When in Fight Flight people will often do things to bleed off energy. You may see someone start to bounce a foot, rock back and forth, or some other movement to release stress.

- Head moves straight up versus tilted

    o A normal head tilt is between 5 and 15 degrees. If someone, in conversation, has their head slightly tilted and suddenly straightens it up in response to a relevant question it is a red flag.

    o Excessive head tilt is commonly a sign of flirting or arousal.

- Increased breathing or changing of the breath rate

    o This occurs because the body is trying to increase the oxygenation of the blood in preparation to fight or flee.

- Sweating
    - This is commonly noticeable on the face and hands. You will often see the person suddenly begins wiping their hands on their legs.
- Trembling
- Blushing

5. Legs and Feet

One reliable indication of what a person is thinking subconsciously often shows up in the feet or legs. While not quite as indicative of a lie by themselves, they commonly provide the hot spot you need to create a cluster.

- Feet pointed to the door

- Suddenly hiding feet under the chair

- Begins raising and lowering of the heels while standing or sitting

- Person, while sitting, stretching or kicking one or both legs out and then brings them back

6. Comforting Gestures

When people are stressed, they tend to do things to comfort themselves. These gestures are often used to self-comfort when responding falsely to a relevant question as well.

- Touching the nose
    - We have erectile tissue in the end of our nose. When we lie in response to a relevant question it engorges with blood making it itch.
- Hand(s) to the eyes partially or completely covering them (hiding something)
- Hand(s) to the mouth (self-hushing)
- Thumb to cheek near the nose (suppressed anger)
- Hand to the brow over one eye while casting gaze down and away (shame)
- Rubbing or placing a hand on the back of the neck
- Covering the neck
- Tongue moving or biting inside of mouth
- Pulling on facial hair
- Taking up less space
- Suddenly crossing arms and legs as a result of a question.

- The person is trying to make himself/herself smaller.

- The person is feeling vulnerable

- Picking imaginary fluff

    - When in Fight/Flight people will often begin to pick imaginary fluff or lint from their clothes

- Adjusting clothing

    - As with picking fluff, a liar will often begin to adjust their clothing, adjusting a collar, shirt cuffs, jacket, or other clothing

- Rubbing or caressing hands

- Playing with rings

- Suddenly begin playing with objects such as a pen or water bottle

Chapter Summary

In addition to the verbal hot spots you learned in the previous chapter, you have now learned about the way our bodies betray us when we lie.

This chapter covered sixty-seven most common physical hot spots you will encounter. There are almost innumerable ways in which our body can betray a lie, but if you can remember both the physical *and* the verbal hot spots you will be worlds ahead of anyone you know.

« Chapter 12 »
Micro Expressions

In addition to the 80+ hot spots we've previously covered, the ability to accurately recognize micro expressions is the most powerful skill you can learn in deception analysis.

What are Micro Expressions?

Micro Expressions are a physical deception class of their own. A micro expression is the leakage of true, suppressed emotion. These expressions flash across the face in less than half a second.

In order to be able to accurately see and understand them requires repetitive visual practice with a micro expression tool as offered by "The Center for Body Language", the "Paul Eckman Group". I've used both of these and highly recommend them. There are a number of others, as well.

Micro expression reading requires that the analyst first be able to recognize the full expression of the seven universal emotions. These emotions, unlike emblematic gestures, are universal across all cultures. Even remote tribes who have never been exposed to the civilized world still demonstrate these seven emotions in exactly the same way.

The Seven Universal Expressions of Emotion

Though we like to think our emotions are complicated they can be distilled down to a few basic emotions. It's important to note that emotions are universal and not cultural as are emblematic gestures. Emotions are displayed the same in every culture around the world.

The seven basic human emotions are:

- Happiness
- Sadness
- Anger
- Disgust
- Contempt
- Fear
- Surprise

Additionally, a person can and often does display a neutral expression when no emotion is present.

While we do have control of these facial expressions in macro, a micro expression is virtually uncontrollable. Often times the person displaying the micro expression doesn't even realize they've shown it.

There are a few situations where micro expressions may not appear when they should, or, they appear to be forced or inaccurate. Two examples are:

- Psychopaths and sociopaths

- A speech that has been rehearsed enough to overcome hidden emotions

A person can also show a neutral expression which makes up the eight primary facial expressions. Keep in mind there can be thousands of different muscular combinations, but these are the primary emotions that drive the expressions.

Types of Emotional Displays

Most people have a difficult time recognizing them all because some are so similar, and they have never consciously considered what the face is doing when expressing an emotion, be it genuine or fake.

For example, in surprise, fear and sadness, the eyebrows all move similarly but once trained, you'll see there are major differences in the muscle groups used to make the expressions.

Happiness and contempt are also very similar, but use different muscle combinations and flexion. Contempt is the only expression that is asymmetrical. In contempt the lip corner is slightly higher on one side. If you see asymmetry in any other expression that's a major red flag that something is going on with that person's emotions.

You will also commonly see a person "masking" in an attempt to hide their true emotions. The most common is a masking smile. Unfortunately for the person masking, if you learn this skill, you'll still see the underlying emotion.

You will often see someone display a "fake" smile while trying to cover any of the other emotions. A contempt smile, for example is very difficult to see because both corners of the lips turn up. However, one side will be only slightly higher than the other.

You will also see other combinations of expressions, or rapid successions of emotions. It is very common to see a person who has "mixed emotions" about something. You may see a flash of happiness immediately followed by contempt, or anger mixed with disgust. There are literally thousands of possible combinations; some that even signal a potential physical or emotional assault.

Chapter Summary

As I stated earlier, micro expression recognition comes only with a great deal of instruction and even more practice. I've watched thousands of practice videos, interviews and interrogations in order to get to my level of proficiency.

If you want to begin learning, one of the easiest ways to see emotions and body language is on television. Start watching interviews with no sound and try to guess what the person is doing with their body and face as you watch, then, rewind the video to see how accurate you may be.

The best way to learn micro expression analysis is by subscribing to an online program designed for that purpose.

The subject of micro expression analysis is too complex and to visual too have covered in this book.

« Conclusion »

To wrap up this book, I would like to thank you for staying with me for the duration. As you've seen and heard, "The Mind Hackers Guide to Detecting Lies" is a fairly comprehensive training tool designed to help you take your communication to a higher level by learning to recognize when someone is lying to you. These skills, once practiced to proficiency will increase your emotional intelligence and empower you to instantly, accurately detect lies so you can find the truth, which means you will be a more powerful and ultimately more profitable communicator.

For booking information to have me present a Keynote speech, a breakout presentation, executive brief, training and/or coaching contact me at:

Phone: 615-388-1389

By email at james@allncom.com

You can follow me on:

FaceBook @ allncom

Twitter @James_G_Springer

Or LinkedIn @jamesgspringer

www.ingramcontent.com/pod-product-compliance
Lightning Source LLC
Chambersburg PA
CBHW021433210526
45463CB00002B/503